I HEARD YOU WHISPER "I Love You"

WRITTEN BY
KATHLEEN TROCK-MOLHOEK

ILLUSTRATED BY
GLORIA OOSTEMA

I Heard You Whisper is imaginatively constructed as two stories in one book: *I Heard You Whisper, I Forgive You* and *I Heard You Whisper, I Love You*. The two stories meet in the middle of the book. Reading the words around the center page turns the book; when the book is closed, the other story begins. The realistic illustrations and text encourage young readers (ages 2-7) to start their own "talks with God."

Kathleen Trock-Molhoek has a passion for children and adults to know God as their Father. She is the founder of Pebbles and Stones (www.Pebblesandstones.com), a ministry that brings the Gospel to children and adults through biblical storytelling, listening, journaling, sharing, and praying in an intergenerational setting. Her teaching model is used in 50 countries. She is the author of *Hiding Places*, *I Love to Pray*, *God Speaks*, and *Kids Love to Pray Too*. A new devotional published through Prayer Shop Publishing will also be available in 2020. She and her husband, Dan, live in Ada, MI.

As a mother of three and a grandmother of nine, **Gloria Oostema** has a special affinity for children. Her simple drawings focus on the gestures and expressions that evoke the emotions of childhood, and her career has focused on projects that point them to God. She has illustrated a number of books for Zondervan including the *God Loves Me Bible*, as well as *101 Favorite Stories from the Bible* for Christian Aid Ministries. She and her husband Jack live in Rockford, MI.

Copyright © 2020 by Kathleen Trock-Molhoek.
All rights reserved. For permission to reproduce anything
from this book, not provided for under the
United States of America copyright law, contact
Kathleen Trock-Molhoek, P.O. Box 625, Ada, MI 49301

Illustrated by Gloria Oostema

ISBN: 978-0-9820844-9-6

Printed in the United States of America

20 21 22 23 24 25 26 27 28   (CHG)   10 9 8 7 6 5 4 3 2 1

Dedicated to Vera Elizabeth Trock

But now I am thinking about you and I just want to say,

"I love you, Jesus. Thank you for my imagination." Exodus 31:3

But now I am thinking about you and I just want to say,

"I love you, Jesus. Thank you for my family." Psalm 68:6a

But now I am thinking about you and I just want to say,

"I love you, Jesus.

Thank you for giving me confidence." Philippians 4:13

Today while I was having fun playing "hide n' go seek,"

I wasn't thinking about you.

But now I am thinking about you and I just want to say,

"I love you, Jesus. You are always with me." Joshua 1:9

Today when I was thinking about you and said, "I am sorry, Jesus! I heard you whisper in my heart, "I Forgive You."

(Close the book and start again)

Today when I was thinking about you  whisper in my heart, "I Love You."

(Close the book and start again)

and shouted, "I love you, Jesus!" I heard you

But now I am thinking about you and I just want to say,

"I am sorry, Jesus. Help me to tell the truth." Ephesians 4:25

Today when I said,
"I don't know who did it?"
I wasn't thinking about you.

But now I am thinking about you and I just want to say,

"I am sorry, Jesus. Help me to be patient." I Corinthians 13:4

Today while I was jumping in front of the line,

I wasn't thinking about you.

But now I am thinking about you and I just want to say,

"I am sorry, Jesus. Help me to listen and obey." Ephesians 6:1

Today when Mommy said I could have one apple, I wasn't thinking about you.

But now I am thinking about you and I just want to say, "I am sorry, Jesus. Help me to be kind to others."

Ephesians 4:32

Today while I was pulling my brother's toy from him,

I wasn't thinking about you.

But now I am thinking about you and I just want to say, "I am sorry, Jesus. Help me to be more thoughtful."

Proverbs 12:10

Dedicated to Vera Elizabeth Trock

I Heard You Whisper is imaginatively constructed as two stories in one book: *I Heard You Whisper, I Forgive You* and *I Heard You Whisper, I Love You*. The two stories meet in the middle of the book. Reading the words around the center page turns the book; when the book is closed, the other story begins. The realistic illustrations and text encourage young readers (ages 2-7) to start their own "talks with God."

Kathleen Trock-Molhoek has a passion for children and adults to know God as their Father. She is the founder of Pebbles and Stones (www.Pebblesandstones.com), a ministry that brings the Gospel to children and adults through biblical storytelling, listening, journaling, sharing, and praying in an intergenerational setting. Her teaching model is used in 50 countries. She is the author of *Hiding Places*, *I Love to Pray*, *God Speaks*, and *Kids Love to Pray Too*. A new devotional published through Prayer Shop Publishing will also be available in 2020. She and her husband, Dan, live in Ada, MI.

As a mother of three and a grandmother of nine, **Gloria Oostema** has a special affinity for children. Her simple drawings focus on the gestures and expressions that evoke the emotions of childhood, and her career has focused on projects that point them to God. She has illustrated a number of books for Zondervan including the *God Loves Me Bible*, as well as *101 Favorite Stories from the Bible* for Christian Aid Ministries. She and her husband Jack live in Rockford, MI.

Copyright © 2020 by Kathleen Trock-Molhoek.
All rights reserved. For permission to reproduce anything
from this book, not provided for under the
United States of America copyright law, contact
Kathleen Trock-Molhoek, P.O. Box 625, Ada, MI 49301

Illustrated by Gloria Oostema

ISBN: 978-0-9820844-9-6

Printed in the United States of America

20 21 22 23 24 25 26 27 28   (CHG)   10 9 8 7 6 5 4 3 2 1

I HEARD YOU WHISPER
"I Forgive You"

WRITTEN BY
KATHLEEN TROCK-MOLHOEK

ILLUSTRATED BY
GLORIA OOSTEMA